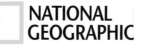

D0100648

# What Plant Is This?

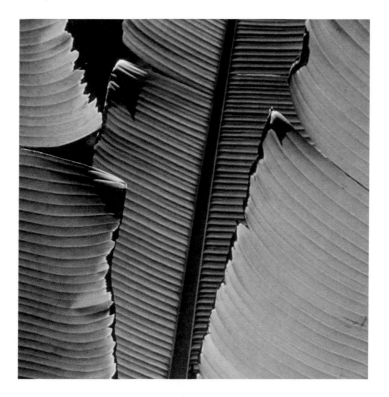

## Leroy Taylor

# What plant is this?

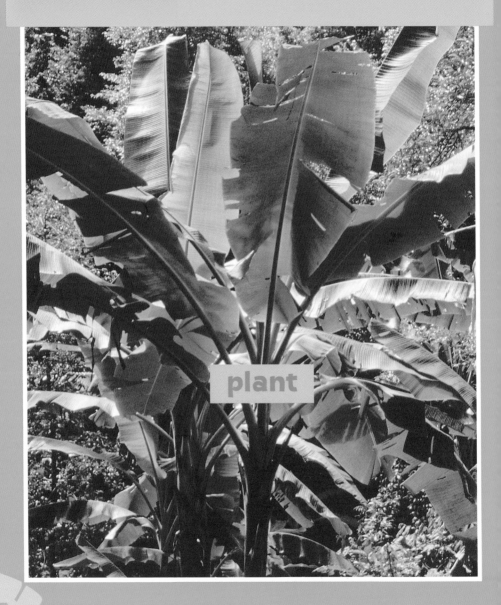

plant

2

# It has **stalks**.

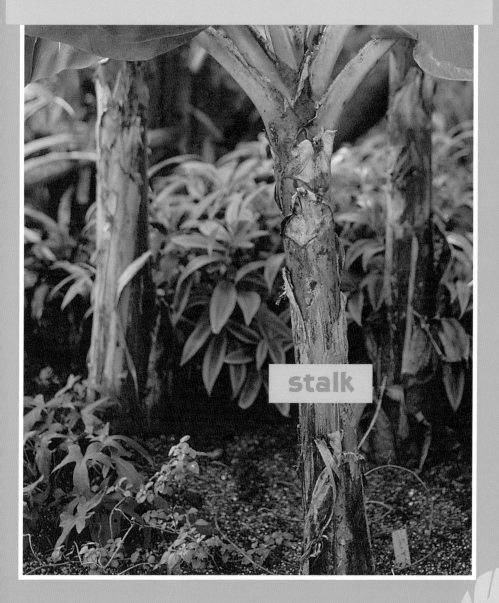

stalk

# It has leaves.

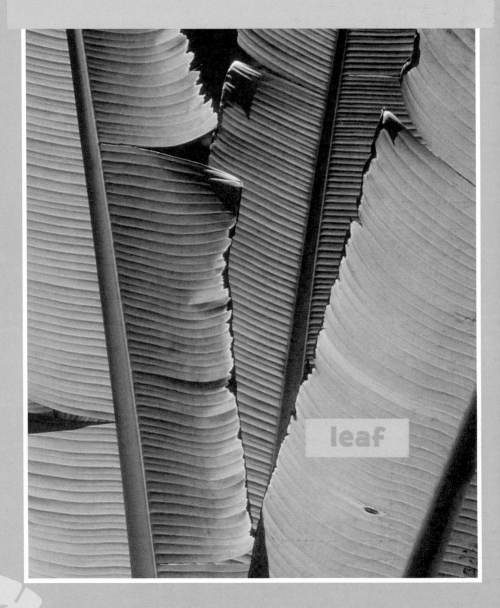

leaf

# It has flowers.

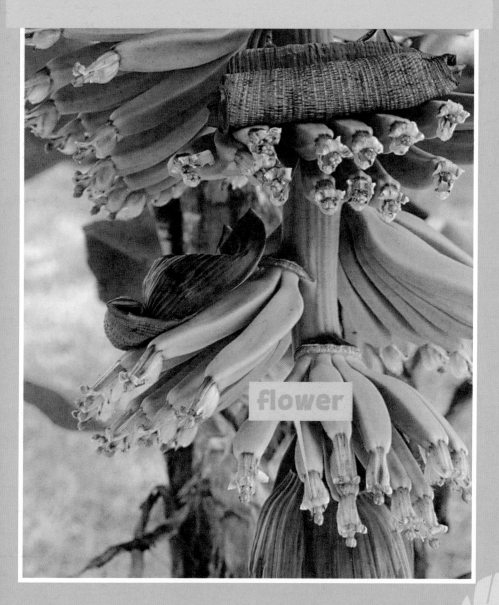

flower

# It has **fruit**.

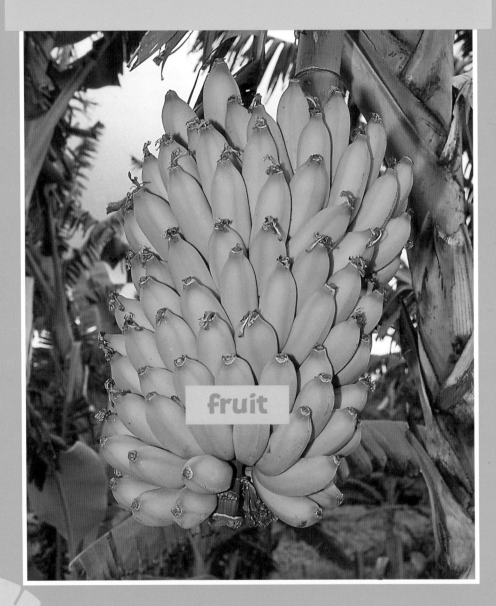

fruit

# It is a **banana** plant.

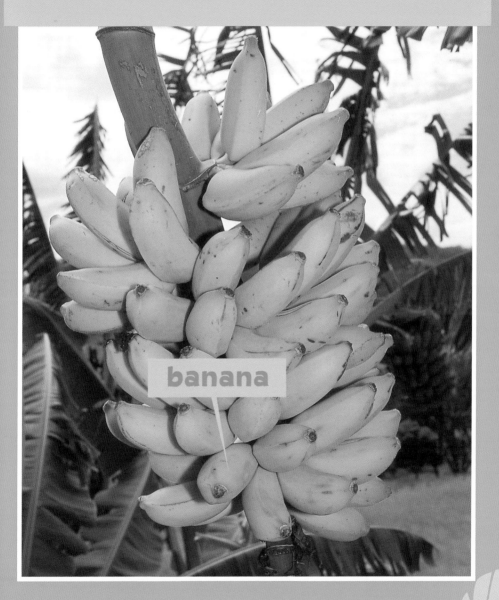

banana

# Yum!

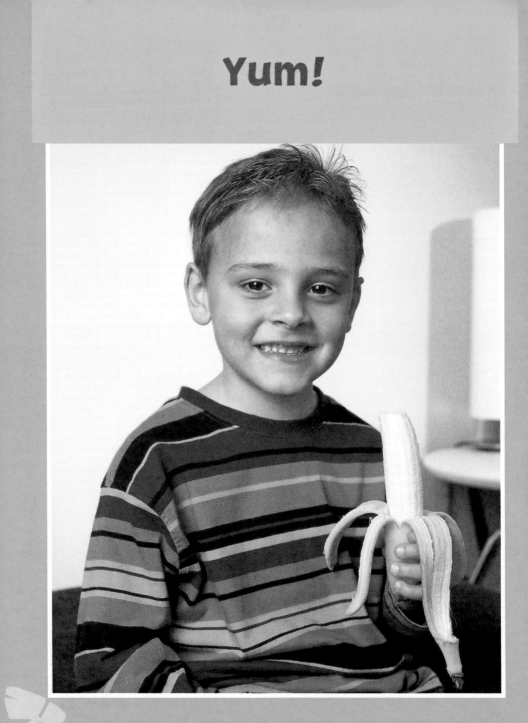